For my friend
Varaz Samuelian
the painter
of the Armenian
spirit
red yellow & black
with admiration,
for tireless work
sincerely
Bill Saroyan
Fresno January 22 1969

my
to the
his

may
4
1965

ian

rk
yan

WILLIE AND VARAZ

WILLIE AND VARAZ

Memories of My Friend William Saroyan

By Varaz Samuelian

536692

Panorama
West Books

International Standard Book Number 0-914330-73-X
Library of Congress Card Catalog Number 85-060101

Published by Panorama West Books
2002 North Gateway
Fresno, California 93727

May 1985

Foreword

Many have written about author-playwright William Saroyan, each as that writer knew Saroyan. Most have known him through his writings and have presented him first as a literary man and second as the man disclosed by his writings. A few may have written biographically about Saroyan through personal contact.

We have here in this work still another biographical account, but one that sees Saroyan as the man himself in his unguarded moments.

Sculptor-author Varaz Samuelian has provided us with this intimate view of the modern bard. At times possibly too revealing, Varaz is honest about it. If an episode—we can call it an escapade—has an embarrassing quality, Varaz himself is just as much involved. Together they were oftentimes two kids on a lark.

The two—Willie, as Varaz knew him, and Varaz, as Willie knew him—were long-time and private friends. Each, an artist in his own way, complemented the other quite nicely as they faced peculiar situations, usually of their own making.

It is the telling of these situations and how "one thing led to another" that makes this work of Varaz' enjoyable and worth-while reading.

Whether it be the capture of tiny frogs in the too-tall grass surrounding Willie's house, or escapades at the Fresno District Fair, these episodes provide the unique insight into Saroyan that a reader cannot get elsewhere.

Saroyan's final days and moments were witnessed only by his

very close friends. And though they came and went, there was a sad loneliness in Saroyan's very last. Varaz was in a position probably better than anyone else to tell about it.

Arra S. Avakian
Fresno, California
January 30, 1985

Former professor of Armenian studies at California State University, Fresno, Dr. Avakian also translated Varaz' Armenian language manuscript into English for this book.

As a painter and sculptor I, Varaz Samuelian, having been a very close friend of William Saroyan for the last twenty years, want to write about our interesting, happy, amusing travels together, and about his tragic death.

Pulitzer Prize winner William Saroyan wrote ninety-four short stories, four plays, six poems, and scores of articles for newspapers and magazines. He also wrote, "Who Is Varaz?," the catalog for my 1965 New York exhibition, which he arranged for me and where I sold not one painting.

William Saroyan called me Varaz, and I called him Willie. I learned to call him Willie from his uncle Mihran, not the Mihran who peddled fruit from his pushcart on the streets of Oakland, but the Mihran Saroyan who owned a women's garment store called the Mona Lisa, on Fulton Street on the mall in Fresno. That Mihran liked Willie very much, and he liked literature. He died in the same hospital in Fresno, Veterans Hospital, eight years before Willie. Whenever I visited Mihran he would always cry and say, "Varaz, I'm afraid I am going to die."

Willie and I always spoke in Armenian. He spoke with a Bitlis accent, with a curious intonation. But he didn't read or write it. When he got a letter from someone in Armenian he would bring it to me to read. But he loved the Armenian tongue. In Paris he had even tried to write a vignette in Armenian, but spelled out in English letters. The effort did not please him and he tore it to shreds.

It is worth writing about this great, talented and interesting

man, this proud Armenian with a giant moustache. He styled his
moustache after the one worn by the popular Armenian hero,
General Antranig Pasha. He saw the general the first time in his
great-uncle attorney Aram Saroyan's office, at the corner of
Fresno and Van Ness. Willie had come to Fresno from San Francisco to get his pay for the work he had done in his uncle Aram's
vineyards. He had not got his money. Aram asked Willie what he

was then doing. At that time Aram was famous as an attorney, and rich.

Willie answered that he wrote. Aram said, "I write, too. I write checks. But what work do you do, Willie?"

"Uncle, I told you. I write books." Aram became somewhat vexed and came back with, "Why don't you tell the truth and say that you are out of a job?"

At that moment Antranig Pasha placed his hand on Willie's head and said, "My son, write. Write. It was the lack of writing that plunged our Armenian nation into the sad plight of these days."

Our First Meeting

I am telling the story of my first meeting with Willie and becoming acquainted with him by taking it just as he wrote it in his booklet, "Who Is Varaz?":

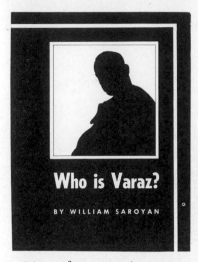

Who is Varaz?

BY WILLIAM SAROYAN

The thing we always want to know about a new painter is, "Is he any good? Where does he stand in relation to the big boys of art of our time? If I buy a painting for $1,000 in 1965, will it be worth $10,000 in 1975? What does his work mean? Is he himself a great man? Is he likely ever to be compared favorably with the enormities of the contemporary world of painting—Pablo Picasso, Mark Chagall, Oskar Kokoschka, for instance?" And so on and so forth. (There are other enormities, of course. As a matter of fact there is no man who paints who is not an enormity. The very biggest enormities tend to be the painters who somehow fail to manage any real fame or any real fortune, unless they marry it, which of course a number of them do.)

Varaz is our painter, the new painter (to us new, to himself not new at all, quite old, as old as the hills of Nairi, so to put it), the painter about whom we may be impelled to ask ourselves some of the classic questions and perhaps a few of the human ones, such as, "Does he ride a bicycle? Does he work for a living? Is he polite? Can he hold his liquor?" And so on and so forth.

Varaz Samuelian, his name in full, born forty-eight years ago in Erivan, the capital of Armenia in Russia, brought up in the vineyard and orchard country surrounding the town, under Ararat, near Arax, the mountain and the river trademarks of the old family and its new members.

Varaz fought in the Armenian Army against the invading Ger-

4

mans, was wounded and taken prisoner, escaped, joined the French underground, joined the American Army, and after the War painted and exhibited in Paris, Barcelona, and Rome, and then came to America.

He stopped for a while in New York, and then in San Francisco, but finally settled in Fresno, where he bought a ramshackle house on San Benito Avenue near O Street. He converted this house and its yard into a studio for the achievement of art, and a place of business—the painting of signs.

On a visit to Fresno from Paris, London, New York and San

Francisco, one day in the spring of 1964, I decided to drive to Armenian Town, to San Benito Avenue where I spent a number of important years of my life. The house at 2226 had long since been demolished, the house that was the scene of my first play, "My Heart's in the Highlands," so I drove on down San Benito Avenue from M to N to O, to have another look at the houses that had survived. On my side of the avenue, the righthand side going east, two blocks up in precisely the same place where my house had been, I saw a ramshackle house. In the front yard was a full standing white statue of the assassinated president, John Kennedy, about five times life-size. Farther back in the yard I saw a huge wood sculpture, more horizontal than vertical, and beyond this work, I saw a very small marble sculpture involving torso, heart, and alphabet, if you can imagine such a work.

As I idled along in the old 1941 Lincoln limousine, as I went past the ramshackle house and yard, I thought, "Now, who the hell in Fresno would be able to do work like that, and willing to set it out in his yard that way?"

Surely an old American, as we used to say, who had retired and taken up work he had wanted to be free all his life to do, perhaps somebody like the Tower-Builder of Watts, but then that man had been an immigrant, from Italy, not an American.

By that time I had crossed O and had turned left on Santa Fe moving north to Ventura Avenue where Guggenheim's Fig and Raisin Packing House had been. From there I figured to move along to the Californian Hotel, pack up, drive back to San Francisco, and in a few days fly back to New York, and then to Paris— but I felt I had left something unfinished, so I swung the car west on Ventura, raced down M back to San Benito, east again and straight up to the ramshackle house, where I got out to study first the statue of Kennedy; and then the wood sculpture—like wave, flame, flower, branch, root, rock, but most of all like form itself; and then the small marble work. All of this among crawling weeds and tall grasses, keeping the place cool and green. I expected somebody to come out of the house, but when nobody did I sat on the front steps, as I had sat so many times at my own house

6

fifty years ago. It was good to sit there, because living stuff was all around. There was an old English walnut tree just at the end of the yard, and across the street in an empty lot there was an abandoned black fig tree, and near it, in the yard of the small house across the street, was a fine apricot tree loaded with the ripening freckled fruit. After a few minutes a barefooted barechested Armenian came out of the red-brick house on the corner, at M Street, holding three tomatoes in his hands. In English he said,

"You like to eat tomato?" In Armenian I said, "Yes, thanks very much, who is the man who has done this work?"

"Varaz. My name is Markar. I am from Erivan, too. I worked for Ford in Detroit nine years. Before that I worked in Stuttgart, in Muenchen, in Hambourg, but now I live here in that red-brick house and Varaz is my neighbor."

"Where is he?"

"Delivering a sign, he'll be back in a few minutes, stay right where you are, he'll take you in and show you the new painting he is making."

"He paints, too?"

"Wait till you see his pictures."

"What do you do nowadays?"

"I saved money, I bought that house, so now my work is that garden, eat another tomato."

"No thanks, but that was the best tomato I ever ate."

"Eat this one, too, I grow so many I need somebody to eat them. Also squash, okra, cucumbers, bell peppers, eggplants, mint, basil, parsley, figs, grapes, apricots, peaches, melons—." Suddenly he roared with laughter. "This is an Armenian place, man."

I ate the second tomato.

"Come along now to the garden for a good cold drink of Fresno water, it is almost as good as the water of Erivan."

"I've always liked the Fresno water."

"You've been here before?"

"From the age of seven to the age of twelve I lived two blocks down the street."

The water was cold and good, and from the garden came the pungent smell of tomato plants, of moist earth, of fruit ripening, of insect, of sun.

A small pickup truck came around the corner of M, and suddenly Markar shouted, "Hey, Varaz, here you are, and here's somebody to see you."

The brakes of the truck screeched, the truck skidded and stopped, the door banged open, and out of the cabin stepped a smiling man of medium height and build, shirtless but wearing shoes.

"Hey, Markar, how are the tomatoes?"

"As true as the paintings." He tossed a tomato to Varaz who caught it but did not bite into it.

"You have it," he said to me.

"I've already had two."

He then ate the tomato, we walked to his house, he unlocked the front door, and we went in. Well, the place was quite simply a place in which a workingman made both art and a living. On the floor was an enormous board on which he was making a picture involving the forms of Armenian dancing. On an easel was a much smaller picture in deep reds and yellows, whose subject I shall permit myself to call **Being**—pure and simple.

Looking, listening, chatting, I thought, "This man **is** an artist. He **lives** art. Other painters teach at universities, but he paints signs for a living. So let me think about Varaz and his art."

I saw everything he had in his studio, and everything in his yard, including back of the house, a couple of tons of metal junk from which he now and then took pieces and worked them into sculptures. He said that at his home, about a mile away, he had many more paintings, and in his garden many works of sculpture. We got into the truck and he drove to his house, in New Armenian Town, near Butler. His French-born Armenian wife brought out brandy and poured while Varaz got out several sketch-books full of drawings. Then we went outside and from a kind of barn he began to bring out paintings and to set them up against the house and fences and trees, and at the same time I glanced at the five or six metal, wood, and stone sculptures among the vines, trees, and vegetables.

We drove back to the ramshackle house on San Benito Avenue. I thanked him, I got back into the Lincoln limousine and drove away.

That was how I became aware of Varaz and his work. Now, I will see if I can answer the questions asked in the first paragraph of this paper:

9

1. Q. "Is he any good?" A. He is very good.

2. Q. "Where does he stand in relation to the big boys of art of our time?" A. He stands a little off from them, more or less alone, but not by any means beneath them, considering his comparative youth, the probability of acclaim soon, his tremendous creative energy, unrest, zest, and compulsion to work.

3. Q. "If I buy a painting for $1,000 in 1965, will it be worth $10,000 in 1975?" A. Yes, and more. How do I know? Well, he is a **painting** painter, but every one of his paintings is a kind of rarity which can never again come to pass in quite the same way—and money **isn't** that way. In fact, money is getting less and less like money, even, while real art always becomes more and more real with time going by. The marvel of it is that with money it is possible to buy art at all, because essentially art just isn't buyable. In a sense, it is always a donation from the artist to the human race.

4. Q. "What does his work mean?" A. It means everything, and I am not being glib. On the contrary. All art means everything, or it means nothing, and that's not being glib, either. In all real art there is the meaning that is in everything—there is the meaning of stuff **itself**, including the stuff of sun and light.

5. Q. "Is he himself a great man?" A. Yes. It would be impossible not to be great and to do the work he has done.

6. Q. "Is he likely ever to be compared favorably with enormities of the contemporary world of painting—Pablo Picasso, Mark Chagall, Oskar Kokoschka, for instance?" A. Yes, because it is possible right at this point in his career to **begin** comparing him favorably with the three named as well as with all of the others, unnamed.

Finally, for myself, I can say that every time I see a painting by Varaz I feel good.

The answers to the other questions.

Yes, he rides a bicycle.   Yes, he is polite.

Yes, he works for a living.   Yes, he can hold his liquor.

William Saroyan

10

William Saroyan was born on August 31, 1908, in Fresno, five houses east of my studio at 2428 San Benito, between N and M streets. That house is now torn down to provide for a highway right-of-way. He spent his childhood in the surroundings of San Benito, N and M, and Ventura streets, and the Holy Trinity Armenian Church.

For a time Willie attended Emerson School, where his teacher was displeased when he came to school after eating garlic. The teacher admonished him, saying that he stunk up the whole classroom with the smell of garlic, and that he should tell his parents not to feed him garlic. But little Willie said that instead of his not eating garlic, the teacher should open the windows.

Willie did not have much formal schooling. His father, who had been a Protestant minister in Bitlis, had come to Fresno where he tried chicken farming at a place about eight miles from Fresno, while at the same time engaging in preaching. He died when Willie was only three.

The Saroyan clan was large. In San Francisco there is attorney Souren Saroyan. A few of the clan changed the name to Sarou-khan, which Willie did not like.

Willie's father, at his death, left four children, two girls and two boys. They were Cosetta, Zabel, Henry, and Willie. Their mother placed the children in an orphanage in Oakland. Willie did not like it. He enjoyed only those days when his uncle Mihran would come to the orphanage with his pushcart full of fruit. His uncle would call him and tell him to take as much of the fruit as he liked. That was the Mihran who in later years came to Fresno and opened a fruit store. Willie and I often went to see him. The store was at Hazelwood and Ventura. He was a good man.

Willie resented his fate. He could not understand why his father had died so young, and why his mother had placed him in an orphanage. He resented the fact also that he was obliged to enter the army.

Willie had always liked books and literature. He did some writing at an early age. He sold newspapers, delivered telegrams, and later wrote for Hollywood movies, finally doing something he liked—writing short stories and plays. During the early period he had a touring theatre together with painter Manuel Tolegian, who played the harmonica beautifully. They traveled from city to city and put on plays that Willie had written. He even had his own theatre in New York.

At the time that I met him he was only writing, and he lived in several places. He had bought a house in San Francisco, on a high hill, at 1823 Fifteenth Avenue, from where he could see the Pacific Ocean. His sister Cosetta also lived there. It was a valuable house. He also had a place in Malibu Beach which he did not live in much. But he spent about six months of every year at his Paris apartment house at 74 Rue Taitbout near Montmarte. He went there in the spring and returned to Fresno in the autumn.

His New York home he had left for his wife, son, and daughter.

William Saroyan was married twice, to the same woman, Carol Marcus, daughter of a wealthy Jewish family. She was very beautiful, and seventeen years younger than he. She was seventeen and he thirty-four when they first married. They had one son, named Aram, and one daughter, named Lousik.

Aram is a writer, involved in literature. Lousik is an actress. At one time Willie told me that she had been with Marlon Brando; they were to play together in a motion picture, so Willie told me.

12

William, Carol and Aram Saroyan in San Francisco in 1947.

After their second divorce, in Las Vegas, Carol Marcus married the famous actor Walter Matthau.

When Willie heard men complaining about women he would say to me that his wife loved big parties, diamond rings, a big house, and Cadillacs. "Five minutes after making love, she would want to do it again, and she wouldn't let me write." For that reason, too, she was very careful about women, and would not let them go near him.

Willie's house was very untidy. There were boxes filled with a variety of published and unpublished books, dusty stacks of newspapers, on the table, underneath, everywhere. Of course, I understand. It was very plain to me. That was clearly the house of a busy artist.

I once asked Willie, "Can you find something you're looking for? My studio and my house are very much like yours. I suffer a lot in trying to find something I want."

13

He answered, "I know exactly where everything is."

My mind went to a story about Chopin's room. A friend had gone there, and with his finger had written on the piano, "I came to see you, but you were out." So thick was the dust that the hand-traced words could be read on the black piano.

That is a simple matter. Artists are so preoccupied with their art that all else is of secondary importance.

Yes, I was saying, Willie did not often approach women. Of course, my observation is about his later years. Once a beautiful woman asked me to tell Willie that she would like to go to his house to clean it, and put things in order as he would like it, and without pay. I told Willie about her. Willie knew her. He said, "No, I don't want it. Women are like that. At first they will do what you want, and then they will make you do what they want."

Of course, before his marriage he was very different, especially when he was working in Hollywood. He drank heavily, smoked, and gambled. When he was drunk he had no knowledge of what he won or lost. I doubt if any girl he wanted escaped from his clutches.

He gambled as though there were no tomorrow. He lost a million dollars. In one night he lost one hundred thousand dollars. His uncle Mihran related the following to me. One morning, at four o'clock, his phone rang. "I lifted the phone drowsily. It was Willie. He was calling from Las Vegas, and he wanted twenty thousand dollars immediately. I told him that I couldn't send him the money immediately because the banks would not open until nine o'clock. I finally wired him the money at ten o'clock. Two hours later the phone in the store rang. I lifted the receiver. It was Willie again. He was now asking for ten thousand dollars, making all kinds of promises that he would return the money in a few days, with big interest."

Judge Ralph Moradian told me this story. When he was writing *The Time of Your Life*, Willie was drinking heavily. The head of a large distillery approached him, asking him to mention his particular brand of alcohol. In the part of the book where customers at the bar ask for a drink, they are to ask the bartender for

14

that brand by name. In return, the head of the distillery would give Willie one case of alcohol each month for the rest of his life. Willie did not agree.

He did the same with the Pulitzer Prize. He did not go to receive the award, which was a substantial sum. Some of our Armenians, ignorant of matters of art and artists, were critical of Willie for not accepting the prize. They reasoned that if he didn't need the money, why hadn't he taken it and given it to the Armenian people, who needed it, or to the Armenian cause!

The Frogs

Around 1962 Willie bought two houses at 2729 West Griffith Way. He bought the places because at that time the houses were completely surrounded by vineyards and orchards. He himself planted fruit trees in front and in back of the houses—peach, pear, plum, fig, etc.

Willie did not like to mow the lawn, either in front or in back. The grass grew tall, and neighbors, as well as city officials, complained because the grass became dry and presented a fire hazard. But he ignored them. He enjoyed walking in the tall grass. His yard was like a wild field. He would say that one should not disturb nature.

By 1974 Fresno had grown. His houses were surrounded by newly built homes. Also a school had been built just a block from his house, where there had been a vineyard. They had also started building a swimming pool and duplexes. But only the foundations had been laid and the swimming pool was just a large hole in the ground. That year July was suffocatingly warm, and heavy rains came. The hole for the swimming pool filled with water, and thousands of frogs bred in it. Most of them swarmed over Willie's fields, among the trees and tall grasses. When one took a step in the yard, five or ten frogs would jump away, and one or two might be crushed beneath the foot.

We had gone into the yard. I wanted to pick plums, peaches,

and figs. After we had picked quite a bit of fruit I said, "Willie, what beautiful frogs you have, hopping all around!"

Willie said, "Varaz, do you want some frogs?" Without thinking I said that I would. Sure, we were going to eat the fruit, but what was I going to do with the frogs!

Willie stopped picking fruit. He went inside and came out shortly with a shoe box and a paper sack. We punched a few air holes so the frogs would not suffocate. So, leaving the fruit picking, we went after frogs. Well, there being a lot of frogs was one thing, but catching them was quite a different thing. Finally, after much shouting, calling, laughing, and cursing, and a lot of sweat, we had caught twenty-two frogs and put them in the shoe box and in the paper sack. We tied the box and bag with old shoe laces. We put the frogs and the fruit in my 1949 Chevrolet pickup and I drove home, laughing and eating fruit.

In 1976 Willie and I were in Helsinki, the capital of Finland. We were starving and entered the lower floor of a two-story seashore restaurant where we ate dishes of all kinds of fish. We had just about finished our meal when suddenly Willie asked, "Say, Varaz, what did you do with the frogs we caught in my yard?" I answered immediately, "What would I have done with them? Of course, I fried them and ate them." He shouted, "No! Varaz, I'm going out. You pay the bill. I'll wait for you."

We Put up David of Sassoun in 1970, in front of the County Courthouse

I completed the twenty-eight-foot high statue of David of Sassoun in 1970. I erected it in the Fresno County Courthouse Park, at the corner of M and Tulare streets. I produced the statue and the foundation all by myself, except for one stone. When I was pouring the cement for the foundation Willie was there. I said to him, "Willie, you place this mountain rock in the cement." He did. The next day he handed me this note:

Passerby, Varaz of San Benito Street made this mighty statue to honor David of Sassoun, the common people, himself, me, and you.

I had lost that note, but found it by chance in 1984.

To celebrate the statue the entire Armenian community, individuals and organizations, had arranged a great banquet in the Convention Center Exhibit Hall. The theatre of the Convention Center complex is now called the William Saroyan Theatre. In 1984 I made the bust of William Saroyan that now adorns the entrance to the theatre.

Willie was the principal guest at the banquet. There too were California Assemblyman Walter Karabian, attorney Paul Mosesian, the Rev. Harry Missirlian, and all the priests of the area. There were 1,800 people in attendance, Armenians and others. The occasion was, however, financially unsuccessful. I had worked on the statue for three years, but I received an amount that was only enough to cover my actual expenditures for materials. It was the first time that William Saroyan appeared at an Armenian gathering.

19

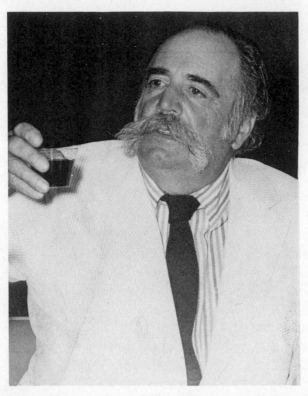

After that banquet we used to have many little gatherings in my house. It was there that Vahe Haig, Ronald Paul, Aram Arax, Donabed Kopoian and his friends, Judge Ralph Moradian, Frank Moradian, Herb Lyon, and many others and their wives became acquainted with Willie.

He was a very interesting person. He spoke magnificently, and held those around him spellbound. He was well-read, traveled in many countries, and was acquainted with many artists and actors. He had been very poor, and very rich. But he never changed. He wore his old clothes, and his shoes had holes in the soles. Notwithstanding the disproportion of his face, the deafness in his right ear, and his crooked nose, when he did wear new clothes he appeared as a handsome, tall, very presentable man. Willie did not dress neatly because he had no time to think about such things. Also, he was a born "bohemian" artist. He knew the position he occupied, and he would never let anyone put him down, or get the better of him, no matter who it was. One evening my wife Anahid and her mother were preparing dinner for a gathering. They were cooking pilaf, okra, eggplant, dolma, green beans, and subereg. All at once Willie came in. My mother-in-law, on seeing him, called out, "Oh, Mr. William Saroyan, I'm very glad to see you. I've heard a lot about you in France and wanted very much to see you and become acquainted."

Willie answered at once, saying, "Now that you've seen me and become acquainted, you will say that it wasn't worth it!"

Later, when the guests had left, my mother-in-law said, "And in truth, it wasn't worth it. He looked like a big, moustachioed Kurd."

We gave parties in our small house and back yard. One day Willie said we should do it more often, but my wife Anahid said she did not like a lot of parties which made too much work for her. She said, "It is not a bad deal—he always comes to our house, but never invites us to his house." We had been invited a couple of times to Frank and Ralph Moradian's houses.

Shish Kebab

I invariably prepared shish kebab for special dinners. I always set it up with interspaced tomatoes and eggplant. When it was time to cook it Willie would leave the guests and stand beside the cooking shish kebab. He liked Armenian foods very much. He had not had an Armenian family life. For virtually all of his life he had lived alone. He would remain by the cooking shish kebab and sometimes pick off a half-cooked piece of meat and put it into his mouth.

Once he told this story. There was a poor Armenian who had been invited to a rich relative's for dinner. The guest had picked off a piece of meat while it was cooking, and ate it, just as Willie was doing. The rich host says, "You know, Gourgen, it's hard to get good meat these days." Gourgen, unmindful, picks off

21

another piece. The rich host says, "The butcher is a friend of mine, and that's how I got this good meat." But Gourgen, still unheeding, picks off another piece, eating it too. At that the rich relative, somewhat vexed, says, "You know, Gourgen, this meat costs four dollars a pound." Gourgen takes still another piece and says, while eating it, "Yervant, four dollars! It's really worth it. It's really worth it."

And I said, "Willie, eat as much of it as you like. However much you eat, it will be worth it for you." It really was worth it.

People knew that I was a good friend of Willie, and they often asked me to introduce them to him. But I was always very careful. I did not offer to do so for most of those who asked. I did not give his phone number, or address, because most of the people would annoy him. Sometimes, when people became acquainted with him they would deprecate him, saying such things as, so what, who is he anyway, his clothes are unkempt, etc. And besides, they stole from his valuable time.

The news of my being Willie's friend had reached Armenia. In 1970 the Song and Dance Ensemble of Yerevan was visiting in Fresno along with the talented poet Vahagn Davtian, and the famous singer Hovhannes Badalian. Vahagn asked me to introduce him to Willie. I took him to Willie's house. Willie already knew him from Iran. And he had heard Vahagn Davtian's name many times. Willie received him enthusiastically, which was an uncommon thing. They spoke for quite a while, about many things. At the same time Vahagn was observing everything— boxes filled with books, the typewriter on the table, papers, newspapers, books, a picture of Martiros Saryan's Masis, a portrait of Willie hanging on the wall, and a few abstract watercolor paintings that I like very much. I pointed them out and said, "You know, Vahagn, these paintings of Willie's are famous works." Vahagn said, "He needs nothing else to become famous. William Saroyan is already world famous for his writings."

Years later I introduced Gevorg Emin to him in Fresno.

*Vahe Haig, William Saroyan, Gevorg Emin and Varaz Samuelian
beneath the statue of David of Sassoun.*

23

A Photographer's
Greatest Wish Is Fulfilled

Fresno photographer Paul Kalinian's long-time, greatest desire had been to photograph William Saroyan. Not long after he made his wish known to me I was able quite quickly to arrange for a picture-taking session in my studio. Paul was able to obtain about twenty photographs. He later converted those photographs into an audio-visual sequence presentation. Here is Paul's story about obtaining the photographs:

How I Shot Saroyan

For many, many years I was fascinated by William Saroyan, not only by his writing ability, but also by his broad forehead, moustache, and his rich impressive image. As a photographer, I wanted to capture his greatness, his natural feelings, and to portray his special genius. However, Saroyan seemed opposed to posing before a camera. After several failing attempts to locate Mr. Saroyan, the opportunity finally came.

One day I discussed the possibility of taking Saroyan's picture with the sculptor Varaz Samuelian. Since Varaz was a close friend of Saroyan, I suggested the idea of setting up my camera and lights in his painting studio in anticipation of a visit by Mr. Saroyan. I was very delighted that Varaz liked the idea.

It was a memorable day when Varaz called on March 26 of 1976 to notify me that Saroyan was in Fresno and might visit his studio. I quickly set up my camera and lights after arriving at Varaz's workshop on the corner of San Benito and "O" streets.

In a few hours, Saroyan arrived on his bike. I was standing behind the unfinished sculptures, rather excited and expectant, while Saroyan and Varaz were hugging and greeting each other loudly yet warmly in a typical Armenian fashion. I wasn't too far from them and although Saroyan saw me, he didn't pay any attention to me.

Not wasting time, I extended my hand and introduced myself

as a photographer. I asked Saroyan if I could take a few pictures of him. "Get lost," said Saroyan.

"But Mr. Saroyan, I . . . "

I tried to explain but my voice was drowned out by his booming reply: "I said no . . . can't you hear? I don't want it."

"But why?" I asked.

Looking straight into my eyes, he replied, "I don't want any pictures taken. You had better forget it." He then turned to Varaz and said, "Who is this man? Why does he insist so much?"

"Willie, he is a good photographer," said Varaz.

After a while Saroyan's attention shifted to various art works. I nodded to Varaz and said quietly, "Varaz . . . listen . . . guide him to your painting room where my camera and lights are set up."

"Okay . . . okay," whispered Varaz. "Be patient, Paul," he continued, "once he begins to know you, maybe you can get some pictures."

Half an hour later when the two of them entered the room, Saroyan noticed I had my camera with me. His face expressed displeasure and uneasiness. "Are you taking my picture?"

I said, "No, Mr. Saroyan, I am just triggering my lights. I don't even have film in my camera."

He came closer and asked me to open my camera. I opened the back of my camera and showed him an empty film holder. When he saw the camera without the film in it, he finally relaxed and sat down on a wooden box-like table in front of my camera. I quickly attached a preloaded film holder onto the back of my camera without his knowledge.

As the moments went on Saroyan gained confidence in me. He also became interested in me and asked me to talk about my native Lebanon. During this interesting and warm conversation I took several pictures of Saroyan.

Then Saroyan asked me to sing an old Armenian song called "Tzangam desnem zim Giligia" which translated into English means, "I wish to see my Armenia." We sang this together, our emotions beginning to swell. It was difficult for him to hold back the tears in his eyes.

25

He wasn't the same man I had met earlier.

"I like you, Paul," said Saroyan. "Take all the pictures you want." I had taken most of my important pictures even before he had expressed his generosity. A few months later, he sent me an autographed copy of *Don't Go But If You Must Say Hello to Everybody.*

—by Paul Kalinian, published in "Ararat," Spring 1984

Photographer Paul Kalinian, far right, took this photograph as well as the ones on pages 27 and 28, and many more of William Saroyan.

27

Thirty-five Thousand
Dollars

In 1969 I taught art at Fresno State College (now California State University, Fresno) and became acquainted with the then president Dr. Ness. Dr. Ness was eager to make William Saroyan's acquaintance, for he had a budget of $35,000 that he could spend on writers in residence. If William Saroyan agreed to be at the college for three months and give a series of lectures, he would receive the $35,000. Dr. Ness asked me to tell Willie about the opportunity. I did so. Willie answered that he was not interested. I tried on another occasion to persuade him. He said, "Varaz, why are you insisting? I told you that I haven't the time."

As usual, in the spring, Willie left for Paris. Dr. Ness was not satisfied with my effort. He telephoned Paris and remade the offer. Willie said that he wasn't interested, that he hadn't the time.

Each fall Willie would return to Fresno from Paris, or wherever he might be, in time for the Fresno District Fair, and for the opening of horse racing. Sometimes he returned earlier in time for the Ringling Brothers Barnum and Bailey Circus.

One such time Willie was standing with his bicycle at 2428 San Benito Avenue at the corner of N Street, in front of my studio. As usual, he had books in his pocket and books tied at the back of his bicycle. Obviously he had just visited the Fresno County Library, which he did often.

"Varaz. Varaz."

I recognized his voice and quickly dropped the brushes I had in my hand and went to open the iron gate of my studio. As usual, we were very glad to see one another. We sang Armenian songs, danced, and inquired about how we were. We cut a chilled watermelon. While he was eating he began to examine intensively the many paintings, the sculpture, and the pieces of iron and wood that were strewn around, here and there.

I began to get ready to go to the horse racing, which was to last only two weeks. I reached in my pocket to see if I had any money. At that moment I remembered Dr. Ness' offer of $35,000. I asked

29

Willie why he hadn't accepted it. "We would now have a lot of money for betting right on the nose, or tail."

"Yes, that's right," Willie answered. "If I had accepted the job I would now be at the college, and we wouldn't now be able to go to the fair to see and bet on the horses."

Amused that the college job had come to this end we happily hopped into my pickup and took off for the races.

Fresno District Fair
and Horse Racing

Before getting into the race track one must first enter the fairgrounds, which are enclosed with an iron fence. There are four gates. The gate we usually used opens off Butler Avenue. One had to buy tickets and drop the tickets into a metal box. The turnstile could then be pushed to turn away, and one would enter. Tickets were priced at two dollars. However, we always got our tickets free. Sam gave them to us. For many years, Sam Naman, an elderly Armenian, had his exhibit of animated animals and people that played musical instruments, danced and sang. The name of some company would be displayed above the exhibit, as sponsor. Sam would receive a fee for setting up his exhibit.

I don't know how Sam got the tickets, but I do know that he always got them for us.

Quickly passing through the poultry exhibit, we would come upon a row of three automatic photograph booths. They were small, with hardly room for two people. One would place himself in front of the camera lens and drop seventy-five cents into a slot. The camera would take the pictures in a second. One would leave the booth, and after about three minutes, three photos would come out of a slot. Every year Willie would have small change in his pocket. He would always drag me into a booth, drop the money in the slot, and afterwards get the three photos. He would cut one off and give it to me, keeping the other two. Willie always liked this. We would have our pictures taken with our heads together like two loving brothers.

We would then go over to the livestock exhibit. The animals would be all cleanly washed, with hair and tails brushed. On display were many kinds and colors of farm animals. There were cows with large, beautiful eyes and white udders so heavily filled with milk that the teats touched the ground. There were steers so fattened that they seemed not to have any bones. There were massive bulls, bellowing, and straining at the chain that tied their nostril ring to a sturdy post, restraining them so that they could not harm people. There were gentle, innocent lambs whose only mission was to provide food for people. And there were goats with their long, slender tails and black beards, bleating incessantly. And there were the stub-nosed swine, with eight to twelve piglets continuously feeding on whatever they smelled or saw, sneezing, wallowing in the dirt and mud, with their tiny twisted tails lying against their rumps.

From there we would go to the arts exhibit where I, too, was a participant with my paintings and sculpture. Virtually every year I would receive a number of awards and also $75 to $150. Then, together with the money I already had, we would be ready for the race track. But we would lose it all.

Then we would visit the exhibits of agricultural machinery, the botanical show, and the display of fruit products. Fresno County is world famous for its fruits, of many kinds, of high quality and superior yield. Fresno is surrounded by endless miles of fruit orchards, vineyards, oranges, peaches, nectarines, figs, plums, almonds, walnuts, pomegranates, pistachios, as well as watermelons, tomatoes, melons, cucumbers, etc. Picture the exhibit hall for fruits and vegetables, arranged with hundreds of boxes of the finest produce, and with watermelons and pumpkins so large that the feet of a child sitting on one would not reach the floor.

This was where we had our greatest fun. We would not leave the exhibit until we had filled our pockets and our jackets with various fruits, taken at appropriate times when the attendant might be looking the other way. Ah, and especially the garlic! Willie said that I should take as much of it as I could. Garlic is very healthful for man.

We would continue on our way, eating the fruit and going through the children's play area to reach the race track, which was also enclosed with a fence. Again, entrance required paying an admission fee. But we were already supplied, thanks to Sam.

The race track spectator stands were long. They rose fifty tiers, covered over. To the left were open stands, with six tiers of wooden benches. There were very few people there. That was where we would go. During the interval after each race we would go over to the covered stands where we would be crowded in with the mob of people of all races and colors. Some in the crowd held newspapers over their heads to shelter them from the sun. Some were offering advice to others, or asking opinions on horses. Some were munching on hot dogs or hamburgers, drinking beer or other cooling drinks. Others, angry, were tearing their losing betting stubs. And still others were studying racing forms and handicappers.

Some were cashing in their winning stubs, while others were standing in line at the betting booths to lay their bets on the next race.

We would go beyond all these people to the end of the stands where about ten minutes before each race from four to twelve horses for the coming race were led. They were magnificent beasts, healthy, tall, slender of leg, strong of muscle, and of all colors, both stallions and mares. They would be saddled there. They were constantly stirring and whinnying. They were the world's most beautiful animals. It was difficult to judge which horse would prevail in a race.

Willie would look them over quickly and go to place his bets. He had made his decision earlier after studying the racing forms. He knew the names of the horses and of the jockeys. He would place his bets based on the knowledge he had.

In later years, as I knew him, Willie drank less and gambled less. But he did drink and gamble on occasion. He was joyous when he won.

In any case, when the races were over, whether we won (which was rarely) or lost, we would be feeling good. We would stop by

33

to see Sam and get tickets for the next day. We would mingle with thousands of happy children and adults, stopping at one of the lunch wagons to buy frankfurters and chili beans (red beans cooked with hot pepper) and ice cream. After eating there, we would start for home.

The Circus

If Willie returned from Paris earlier we would go to the circus, which played in Fresno for a week. It was, of course, a traveling circus, going from city to city. In Fresno it played at the Convention Center Selland Arena, at the corner of Ventura and N, two blocks from my studio at 2428 San Benito. On the grounds outside the arena they set up tents for the horses, elephants, donkeys, camels, llamas, and zebras, as well as small and large dogs. Vicious animals, such as lions, tigers, jaguars, and bears, were kept in cages. I would often hear their growling or roaring, and the whinnying of the horses, from my studio.

Sometimes Harold Markarian would be with us, and also Archie Minasian, who was Willie's cousin.

When I went to the circus I always took along my sketch pad and made drawings. Willie always watched me, but said nothing, except on occasion. "There are more ropes and trapezes and lights than animals. You never sketch the apparatus of the circus."

Willie laughed like the children. He asked them questions and listened to their answers. He ate popcorn and ice cream sandwiches. He drank Coca Cola. He applauded every act. He always had a good, good time.

35

The Gleaners

We often went into the vineyards to gather fruit. We would park the auto alongside, dash into the vineyard, pick quickly, get back into the car and drive off. In the fall, especially after the grape harvest, we would go into the vineyards, now variegated, and tread over the fallen red and yellow leaves, making a crunching, rustling sound. We would glean the left-behind, now golden bunches of grapes of unbelievable sweetness. We picked figs that had ripened fully and fallen to the ground, sweeter than those taken from the tree. We filled bags and carried them home.

We often went to farms with Bak Makasian because Willie wanted to buy a farm and build a home and museum.

Sometimes we would go with Harold Markarian and Frank Moradian. Frank had said to me that whatever money Saroyan might need, he could provide it. But Willie told me that he didn't want one cent from anybody, that he wanted to build his museum through his own means.

Willie often came to my studio on his bicycle carrying two peda and two lavash breads for us to eat. He would get them from Valley Bakery nearby, from Janet and Sam Saghatelian, good friends of ours. They were the owners of Valley Bakery, which was on Santa Clara Avenue, only a block from my studio.

Willie came to see me many times at my studio when it was 100

Valley Bakery at Santa Clara and M in Fresno.

37

to 108 degrees, Fresno hot weather. First he drank water from the faucet in his hands even if I had dirty glasses covered with paint and clean glasses, too, near the faucet. Then he would sit in a cool spot on top of a low wooden box, and I would bring grapes and watermelon, peaches or other fruits from the refrigerator, and with lavash bread that he brought from Janet, we would sit and eat together. I sometimes did sketches with pencils or painted with oil, drawing academic or abstract paintings, and we would talk about the Armenians. He told me about Hollywood and about different actors and world affairs. Once in a while he took a pencil and paper or cardboard and drew pictures.

Willie last brought his son Aram to my place sometime about 1975. Aram was already a matured, tall, dark-eyed, handsome young man. I liked him at once. After we had chatted for a while and looked at some paintings in my studio, I said to Aram, though I don't know why, "Aram, respect your father. He is a great man, a great writer, a literary person. We Armenians and people of all nations who have read his books like him. He is an experienced man. Listen to your father." I think Aram did not like what I said, nor did he like my untidy studio. After remaining a little longer they hurried off.

My Friend
and My Neighbor,
Markar and Barsegh

Once when Willie came to my studio we were picking lemons from my relative and neighbor Markar's yard. My neighbor Barsegh, on the other side, was cursing, and very angry at his daughter. Willie asked me why that man was so angry. I said that I would find out. I went over and asked Barsegh what had happened. He said that his girl had for three nights come home at twelve or one o'clock. "She's found some tramp I've never seen. I don't know who he is. She's fallen in love with him and they make love." I got some grapes from Barsegh and returned and told Willie, who was still picking lemons. Willie wanted to know how old the girl was. I said that she was about twenty-two or twenty-three. Willie said, very much unmoved, "Of course she has to make love. That's natural. Why should the father be angry? He should be angry if she doesn't make love."

I was just then reminded of a joke, a 1934 Polos Muguch joke, from my birthplace. During those years Armenia was suffering from a shortage of bread, sugar, tea, and other foods. It was possible to buy them only with coupons, which were issued according to the size of the family. Polos Muguch was a thin, tall man from Gumre. He was like a telephone pole. One day he comes home and finds his wife and daughter wailing loudly that they have lost it, lost it, lost it. He asks his daughter what it is that they have lost, and why they are crying. The two do not answer, but continue their wailing. He begins to lose his patience and angrily demands that his wife tell him why they are crying. Finally, the wife says that their daughter has lost her virginity. Polos Muguch takes a deep breath of relief and says, "You stupid woman, you nearly gave me a heart attack. When you were wailing about losing it I thought you had lost our food coupons."

I told Willie the joke. He laughed and said, "That's just the way it is."

The Meeting of
Michael Arlen and Saroyan

About 1975 Michael Arlen, Jr., came to my studio. We talked for quite a while. At that time he was writing the book *Passage to Ararat*. I saw from his comments that William Saroyan had been his ideal, from the very beginning, notwithstanding that his own father had been a writer. A little later Willie came and we all went together to an Armenian concert at the Convention Center Theatre. Willie, Michael Arlen, and all of us were much pleased with the concert. While we were talking I said that it would be good if he, Michael Arlen, changed his name back to his original Armenian name, Michael Kouyoumdjian. He did not approve of my suggestion.

Journey to Yerevan

William Saroyan had been invited to Armenia by the Committee for Cultural Relations with Armenians Abroad. He said to me, "Let's go together." I said, "Good idea. Let's go." In 1976, with the help of Margo Ohanesian and Mr. Minchuk of the Soviet Consulate in San Francisco, we got our visas. We arranged everything in the course of one week. We bought our tickets and set off from Fresno on September 28. Willie took his typewriter, some paper, and a few items of clothing. I took quite a few gifts, for my brother's and sister's children and grandchildren. Our first flight took us to Los Angeles. We had hardly descended from the plane when we heard a loud paging, "Mr. William Saroyan. Mr. William Saroyan." We waited near the plane. Shortly, an automobile drove up. A beautiful girl placed our bags in the car and we got in. We were transported directly to where our next flight would depart. We would be off for London, Helsinki, Leningrad, Moscow, Kiev, and Yerevan.

While waiting in the airport I bumped into an Armenian who

40

had come from Armenia. I wanted to introduce him to Willie. He said that could it be that this was indeed William Saroyan? "You know what a famous man William Saroyan is. The people of Armenia like him very much. They honor him." That man couldn't believe that it was William Saroyan himself.

Willie was dressed in very ordinary clothes. If you didn't talk to him and hear his booming voice, you would never distinguish him from any ordinary man with a big moustache. That would be especially so if you saw him pick up discarded newspapers thrown into a trash bin, or from under a table. He would stuff the papers under his arm, or in a pocket. His pockets were always filled with papers and books. He read incessantly, and rapidly, whatever he came across.

We finally boarded the aircraft and took off for London. At the London airport we suddenly came upon David Niven. Willie introduced me to him. They went into a bar, and I followed them. They talked enthusiastically about Hollywood, about Clark Gable, Gary Cooper, James Cagney, Mickey Rooney, Rosemary Clooney. Of course, it was Rosemary Clooney who became very famous when she sang "Come-on-a My House," that Willie wrote. Ross Bagdasarian wrote the music. Willie and Ross made a lot of money.

Willie knew all the famous actors. After David Niven had one drink he left us. Willie told me that it was he who had introduced Charles Chaplin to his last wife, who lived with him until his death, in Switzerland.

Willie told me that once George Bernard Shaw had asked him to visit him. Willie had gone, and left very much impressed with the man. "He was a saintly man, like Jesus Christ."

Willie told me that it was not his fault that he had had an argument with Hemingway. This is the way he explained it. "I had gone into a bar in Paris with Steinberg. Hemingway was there, drinking with some friends. When he saw Steinberg entering with a cane in his hand, he arose at once and snatched away the cane. He struck it against his knee and broke it. That was the way the quarrel started. I interceded, to separate them. But apparently I had been drinking and it was in that way that I got into the fight and my nose was broken."

It didn't work out right in 1935 either, when he went to Yerevan and couldn't see the important writers. "I was hardly able to find **Charents Vahan Totovents, Gourgen Mahari, and Zabel Yessayan**," he told me. "They said that they had to go to Moscow to attend a Soviet Union Congress of Writers. They were just leaving. I found them in Moscow."

Willie told me that he was a friend of Arshile Gorky. They used to talk about abstract art.

It was time for our flight. We boarded the aircraft, and when we reached Helsinki it was already evening. Willie went to take a nap. I went into the city to buy fruit. The next morning we roamed Helsinki's streets and found the hotel where he had spent the night in 1935 and the music store where he had got the address of Jean Sibelius. He had gone to visit Sibelius and become acquainted with him.

Notwithstanding that a strong, cold wind was blowing, we continued roaming the streets. I was walking briskly and getting ahead of him. I would then turn back to join him. The wind blew off my hat many times, and I would chase after it to catch it and put it on again. Then once again the wind would catch it and blow it off. All this amused Willie, and he would laugh. He said, "Varaz, that's not a hat you're wearing. It's a bird. It doesn't want to stay on your head. It wants to fly away from you." He said he would write "The Flying Hat."

We reached the seashore. There was an open-air market where everything was being sold. There were a dozen or more large and small boats. After walking about we entered a restaurant at the seashore and had a meal consisting of a variety of fish.

We remained in Helsinki for two days and saw a lot—old and new buildings, picture galleries, and many large and small statues.

As we were standing in a public square we saw a group of about ten people, men and women. I asked a young, pretty Finnish girl, in Russian, how to get to our hotel because we were lost.

She knew Russian and she gladly showed us the way. After chatting with her for a few mintues I said that we were to leave this beautiful city of Helsinki the next day and fly to Leningrad. She said, "Oh, no. No! Don't go there. If you do, they'll murder you." I said there couldn't be any such thing. She left us quickly.

I was reminded then of a joke. A Catholic Italian born in America goes to a Jewish barber for a haircut. The Italian says to the Jewish barber, "You know, I'm going to Italy on a trip. I'm going to visit Venice, Milan, Rome. And I'm going to visit the Pope at Saint Peter's." The barber says, "Hey, don't go to Italy. They're all robbers and thieves there. They'll steal all your money and your clothes. The hotels are dirty, and overrun with rats. The food is rotten and expensive. The spaghetti and pizza has no taste. And they'll never let you see the Pope. Etc., etc." The Italian is gone for two months. Then suddenly he appears at the Jewish barber's. The barber asks, "Where have you been all this time?" The Italian answers, "Well, you should know. I went to Italy and everything was wonderful. I visited Milan, Verona, and Venice, which is all built on water. You travel there only by gondola, along the canals. I went to Rome. I saw the Coliseum. At Saint Peter's I saw the paintings by Michaelangelo and I saw the Pope and kneeled before him. The Pope put his hand on my head and blessed me. Then he bent over and whispered in my ear." The barber asked what the Pope had whispered. The Italian answered, "He said, 'What a lousy haircut you have!'"

It was time to fly to Leningrad. When we were to leave the hotel we went to the cashier to pay our bill, but the cashier said our bill was already paid. I asked Willie why he had already paid. He said he had a credit card.

Writer Levon Mkrtichian and the young poet Razmik Davoian were waiting for Willie in Leningrad. It was already night when we arrived. They took us to the Astoria Hotel facing on Isacov Square. I don't know why Willie wanted to stay at a different hotel. But where he wanted to stay the rooms could be paid for only with cash dollars. However, neither Willie nor the others had the money. It was midnight, and Willie was insisting on staying at that hotel. Otherwise, he said, he wanted to be taken back to the airport to return home. But it was good that I had some money. I paid for his room as well as mine, and it was quite a lot.

The next morning we walked along Leningrad's beautiful streets. We passed the Hermitage Museum. Because there were many people standing in line waiting to go in, Willie did not want to wait, so we did not go in.

We took a boat trip along the Neva River and saw many beautiful sights.

When we were walking along Nevsky Boulevard Willie said, "Anyone who walks along this way should be proud because Gogol, Pushkin, Dostoevsky, and Turgenev walked here." He was happy there, especially so, with his love for Armenian things, when we were taken to the Caucasian Restaurant. There we met a man named Garik, from Yerevan. Garik worked at night; during the day he attended the university.

The next day we went to visit the Peskarev Monument. It had been built in memory of the defenders of Leningrad during World War II. One hundred thousand Soviet citizens lost their lives in the defense of Leningrad.

It was already evening. The grey, lyrical clouds of Leningrad were hanging low over the memorial, which is a perpetual witness to that terrible war. The memorial consists of ten or more large and small statues and clusters spread along a 500-foot-long stone base. On it is written, "No one and nothing is forgotten." There is also a text from the diary of an eight-year-old girl who had died. Her whole family had died. "Savichev died. They all died," said her diary.

Willie and the others were sad as they viewed the memorial statues. But for me, there were tears in my eyes, unseen by other eyes. The six years of tragic war suddenly leaped before my eyes. I had seen the war without shedding a single teardrop. I was a dedicated soldier, wounded, starved, a skeleton, sick, a prisoner in the fascist German prisoner of war camp. I too had defended Leningrad, but on a different front.

44

My aunt's son Edward had been killed in one of Leningrad's streets while defending the city.

Levon introduced the director of the memorial to Willie. The director presented Willie with a large silver medal from his office, as a souvenir of the visit. It was dark by the time we left. I felt that Willie had been very much satisfied, and also deeply moved, by the visit.

The next morning we again went for a walk along Leningrad's streets. Willie admired the old and new buildings, and the churches. He always stopped when we came to a book store. In one store he saw a book of Sylva Kaputikyan's poems, which he bought. Walking along Nevsky Boulevard we were happy, singing Armenian songs.

We boarded a train for Moscow.

Moscow

In Moscow Willie met many writers and became acquainted with Ozerov, who was president of the Soviet Writers' Union, as well as editor of the Russian monthly "Voprosi Literatura" (Questions in Literature). The monthly "Druzhba Narodova" (Friend of the People) had written about William Saroyan along with Sergei Barouzdin and Freda Lourein.

Moscow knew William Saroyan. The next day we visited the Tretakovyan Gallery. Willie walked through the chambers rapidly, but he did stop and look long at some paintings. Later, on Willie's wish, we were taken to sculptor N. Nigoghosian's home and studio. He was an industrious and fine man. Secretary Krushchev had commissioned him to produce about twenty statues of men and women to adorn a large government building. He later showed us a fine sculpture of an old woman. Someone said that an American had offered $50,000 for that statue. But he had not been permitted to take it away.

At that time many Armenaians were emigrating from Armenia. One of the group complained that visitors would come and give misleading promises to Armenians, causing many to leave their homeland. He said that it wasn't possible for anyone to offer so much money for a statue. That started a bitter argument. Then Willie interceded and calmed them. "What are you fighting for?" he asked. "God grant that someone offers a hundred thousand."

The next day we went to Peredelkino, which was two and a half hours distant from Moscow by auto. It was a summer resort for artists, situated in a forest. There we visited Boris Pasternak's grave, under a large evergreen tree. There was a small stone. It was covered with snow, which we wiped off. Written on the stone was "Boris Pasternak"—a simple stone for a great man. He wrote *Doctor Zhivago*. About three paces away was the grave of Vera Zvyaginskeva; the stone was a beautiful khachkar (an elaborately carved large stone stele bearing handsome crosses and designs) from Armenia.

We were walking in the forest over the snow and came upon a small, very old church, which was very dark inside. There were ten or so elderly Russian Christians praying by candlelight.

It was cold. We went to writer Artarova's house. She received us very warmly. She entertained us with hot tea and some refreshments found in the house, which apparently was a hut built during the reign of Empress Catherine.

Levon asked Willie to enter something about Russian writers in his notebook. Willie wrote, "Lev Tolstoy, Dostoevsky, Chekhov, Turgenev, Gorky, Gogol's "Shinel." Pushkin is magnificent. In poetry he is a giant. It is hard in a few words to write about great Russian writers.—William Saroyan."

Willie often went for walks alone in Red Square. He visited the churches, the Kremlin, and the graves of the leaders of the October Revolution placed along the Kremlin wall. Thousands of people were walking about here and there in the Square. And thousands had queued up in a long, winding line to view Lenin's Tomb.

The next day we boarded the plane and flew to Kiev. After waiting around in the airport in Kiev for four hours we boarded the plane for Armenia.

In the plane Levon told us some jokes about the czar and also read some of Nahapet Kouchak's quatrains translated by Osers. Razmik recited some poems he had written. Willie listened. He was interested, and pleased.

I would introduce Willie to various people in the plane, but he was not pleased with that. He did not want people to know who he was so that they would not be hesitant in speaking to him, but rather express themselves without restraint. He would ask questions in his booming voice, hundreds of them, in rapid-fire sequence.

The pilot of the plane was Armenian. He invited Willie to ride in the cockpit. The plains of Ararat and the mountain itself could be seen much more clearly from there. The pilot made an extra turn around Yerevan to afford a better view of the city. When Willie came out of the cockpit he was sad, because the Ararat he had been admiring did not belong to Armenians any longer.

The aircraft circled and descended slowly into the airport of Yerevan, the capital of verdant and rocky Armenia, my birthplace.

There at the airport, awaiting William Saroyan's arrival, were the television crews, the radio people, and a large group of talented Armenian writers and poets—Hovhannes Shiraz, Sergei Khanzadian, Vahagn Davtian, Sylva Kaputikian, Maro Markarian, Vartges Petrosian, Gevorg Emin, Levon Miridjanian. Vartges Hamazaspian, president of the Committee for Cultural Relations with Armenians Abroad, and Antranik Martirosian were also there. We were taken to the Armenia Hotel. Willie's beautiful room opened up on Lenin Square. On the table was a bouqet of flowers from Yerevan's hills and fields, and a large tray filled with a variety of fruit.

I had been left unattended at first. I was later taken to my brother Artavasd's house. His son, Yuri Samuelian, is a fine sculptor. Lovik is a coach in sports. His daughter is Lousik.

In Yerevan we met writer Levon Miridjanian. He had been in America, and in Fresno, where he had met William Saroyan. We went together to the Sundukian Theatre of Yerevan where we

saw a presentation of Willie's "My Heart's in the Highlands."
Staging was by V. Ajemian. The incidental music was by the talented Arno Babajanian.

Willie was well satisfied with the performance. It was the first
time that I saw him go up on the stage after the performance and
appear before the audience. He was generously applauded for
his successful play.

Normally, he did not attend a presentation of one of his plays
when it was staged by someone else. And if he did go, he went
incognito, so no one would know him. He would sit in a far-off,
dark corner during the performance. When lights were turned on
for the intermission he would slip away. He would say to me,
"They mutilate my writings. Only I should stage my plays."

Once the well-known movie actor Mike Connors (Krikor Ohanian), who played the role of "Mannix," asked Willie if he would permit the staging of one of his plays for television, in which he, Mike Connors, would play. Willie had answered that that would be possible only if he himself could stage it. And he did not agree to it.

Once, in 1973, we went together to the Hartford-Huntington Theatre in Hollywood to see "The Time of Your Life." The actors were well known, and I thought that the staging was very successful. I liked it altogether. But Willie had been very much annoyed that a few things had been changed, and that he had been told that the lead roles would be played by Henry Fonda and Jane Fonda, when in fact they were not. Generally, he would not allow commonplace actors take on roles in his plays.

The next day after seeing "My Heart's in the Highlands" we saw the three-act comedy by Armashan Papayan, "The World Is Topsy-Turvy," staged by V. Ajemian, with sets by painter Arouchian. Willie enjoyed it. He laughed continuously.

The next morning we were invited to Armashan Papayan's house to have porridge (boiled meats). Marshal Bagramian was there too. We had an interesting conversation about war. I remained steadfast in my conviction that everything was in the hands of the military, that mankind's greatest enemy is war, and that it is necessary to war against war.

Levon Miridjanian led us to the village of Nahapet Kouchak, where we heard the story of his life, and where many of his quatrains were read and recited. In the evening we had recitations from Parouyr Sevak, Charentz, Vahan Derian, and Hovhannes Toumanian. Young men and women sang village folk songs. They had the genuine flavor of the village. In all my life I had not heard such splendid songs. I felt that villages should remain villages. It was there that our Armenian language and customs were preserved, remaining free from foreign influences. I marvelled. I love the Armenian village.

We dined on village foods, delicious tonir-baked bread. On leaving the village I saw many brooms stuck into the rooftops of houses. I learned that it was a custom in that village to display the broom in the rooftop if there was a marriageable girl in that household. There were so many, it seemed each family had a marriageable daughter.

They gave William no peace. He was grabbed by one and then another. Later we went to a banquet for members of the opera. Willie was in ecstacy, hearing their singing and recitations. He joined in some of them. He was having a magnificent time.

Every day different writers took him to different places— Zangezour, Meghri, Garni, Sevan, Etjmiadzin, Zvartnots, various memorial monuments, schools. They had him plant trees here

and there with his own hands. He chatted with children. He told them stories, and listened to their comments. I believe that those few days were among the happiest days of his life.

During the last two years of his life it seemed some things were bothering him. He was beginning to forget things. There were troubling thoughts in his mind which he was unable to resolve himself. One or two times he forgot and left money in his laundry. He waited for the laundry to be returned. He looked for his socks, not remembering where he had put the money.

Once I told him a joke. A half hour later he told me the same joke when there were some of our wealthy friends nearby.

This was the joke.

A rich photographer of peaceful things such as flowers, trees,

streams, etc. approaches a poor painter who has suffered all his life to produce his art. The photographer says to the poor artist, "You know how great our creativeness is, and how valuable we are to mankind." The poor artist then relates a tale. A hen approaches a pig and says that the two of them are very beneficial to mankind, by producing bacon and eggs, between them. The pig answers that, yes, they are beneficial to mankind, but there is a difference. "You give up the egg that you lay, but I have to give up my life to produce the bacon."

When Willie told that story I broke down with laughter, not because of the joke itself, but because he was telling my joke to those about us, trying to get a point over to our wealthy friends.

The Simple, Beautiful Girl
with a Liberated Mind

One day we were walking through the campus of Fresno State University. We came upon a beautiful young girl, about nineteen or twenty. She was evidently a very liberated person. Virtually all of her bosom showed under her blouse, like two cantaloupes. She came up to Willie and said, "I would like very much to have sex with you. What a fine union and issue we would have, with your bright, creative mind, and my fresh, beautiful body." Willie smiled and said to the beauty, "It's quite true that the blending of my mind and your beauty would make a fine union, a very beautiful whole. But this is not the right time for my present body and your present mind to unite. You are twenty years too late."

On hearing that, the young girl turned and left us. I nearly went crazy.

I was reminded of a famous event. George Bernard Shaw had received a letter from a beautiful woman from America. She wrote that she had read his writings, which she admired. "Your writings and your mind and your creativeness are magnificent. I would like to marry you. Imagine what splendid children we would have from your mind and talent and my beauty." Shaw had answered, saying, "Yes, if it turned out as you say, but if it turned out the opposite, and the child is born with my beauty and your mind!"

Willie was beginning to feel not so well, although he never spoke of it. I would ask, "Willie, my friend, how are you?" He would answer that he was well, and never spoke of his illness. But I felt it. I knew that something was wrong with him, burning inside of him.

Once in Paris he had lost a lot of blood. We went to a hospital. The doctor wanted to give him a transfusion of blood, but first needed to take some to determine his type so that the proper blood could be given. But Willie objected and refused to allow it. We left the hospital. He did not generally use medicines. He feared and lacked confidence in physicians, especially surgeons.

Years later Gail Sarkisian, who worked at the Fresno Veterans Hospital, said to him that the doctors had great hope that an operation would be successful. At that time the growth was very small, and had just started. But he feared the operation and would not allow it. He would remain in the hospital one or two days, and leave, believing that he could cure himself by eating nothing, or eating very little, and by drinking tea.

Many times we spent hours going from store to store to find the tea he wanted. There were dozens of kinds. He would say that tea is the most beneficial food for man. "Drink it, Varaz," he would advise me. He always served me tea in cups that had blackened from tea. Never mind that the blackening came from hot tea; even the iced tea blackened the cups.

The tea kettle was on the stove, warming, morning till night. He held a cup of tea in his hand. He typed standing. He drank probably thirty cups of tea a day.

*Willie and Varaz with Beverly Ohanesian
and Archbishop Serovpe Manukian.*

He had pretty much given up smoking and alcoholic drinks, but he had become addicted to tea. In private dinners he did drink. He ate well and enjoyed himself.

A few times Bishop Serovpe of Paris came to Fresno. He was Gail Sarkisian's cousin. He stayed at the Sarkisian home. Willie and I would visit the Sarkisians, and Gail would try to persuade Willie to undergo surgery. But he still refused. Gail still insists that if Willie had undergone surgery earlier he would have lived longer. I asked Dr. Artin Jibilian, a physician friend, about the wisdom of having the surgery. He said to me that the growth had consumed the entire bladder, and that there was nothing left to be removed surgically. "And Willie's head is somewhat affected."

Willie's Pride

Willie was one who would never let another prevail over him. He would not give a moment of his time to someone he did not want to talk to. If such a person, in some manner, got his telephone number and phoned him, he would instantly hang up. He did not like wealthy people. He always said that they want to take advantage of people with their money. He would not give any opportunity to promoters of new products even to talk to him. He said they asked silly questions. He did not want his name to be spread about.

It made no difference to him who it was who wanted to contact him, government officials, wealthy people, old acquaintances who had for some time broken contact with him, a neighbor. If he were in an angry mood, and his own son appeared, he would even go across the street to avoid greeting him.

The City of Fresno wanted to change the name of Emerson School to the William Saroyan School. He would not allow it. He said that using the name of a living person was wrong. But after one had died, and he was worthy, that was a different thing.

Sometimes he would try to get ahead of others; yet, at other times, he would let everyone go ahead.

Once we were waiting in line at an Armenian banquet, to enter the hall. Someone had come to escort him to his place ahead of the others. He refused to go, saying that he was an ordinary person like the others, and he would stay in line.

He was like that. He might refuse to talk to famous and important people. And then you would see him stopping to talk to a peasant, an ordinary person, a drunk, a hobo, or a poor beggar. He could spend hours talking to them. He would say that there are no important, indispensible people. "They are all the same."

He was the same with money. He would filch a five or ten-cent piece of candy from a store. Or, he would put twenty-five cents in a newspaper dispenser and when the lid opened he would remove two or three copies. He would argue over a few dollars with some people. Many of his acquaintances would say he was a stingy man. Yet, he would lose thousands in gambling, and he had the means to earn thousands with little effort, or to exploit others, which he did not do.

For example, one day a large automobile dealer asked me to tell William Saroyan that they had a latest model of an automobile and that if he would sit in it and allow them to photograph him in the car, which photo they would use only for their establishment, they would give him the car. At that time the car was worth from five to six thousand dollars. They gave me a letter to give to Willie, making the offer. I related the whole to Willie and gave him the letter. He said, "No! Are they crazy?" He didn't even open the letter, but sent it back.

He had separated from his wife. He spoke and wrote unkind things about her. Yet, he was still in love with her, and for that reason he never married again, although he had many opportunities to do so.

It was the same with his son and daughter. As far as I know, he was virtually always quarreling with them. But he loved them, and especially his grandchildren.

Besides having a very ordinary human nature, William Saroyan was a genius. He was an anthropophile. He sought peace. And most of all, he regarded writing as the most important aspect of his life. He was serious in writing. He considered himself one of the world's greatest writers. For example, a young but famous Armenian poet once said to him as they were riding in an auto in Moscow, "William Saroyan, you are a genius." Willie answered immediately, saying, "Of course I'm a genius. There is no one in the world like me. You cannot become like me." I said to the youth that he was young, and that if he worked and learned, he, too, like William Saroyan, would become great. But the youth insisted that that could not be. "I cannot become a genius like him."

Of course, there are many who know their worth, and openly claim their superiority over others. One such is the painter Salvatore Dali. He lives in a palatial home and says that he is the king of kings. He actually regards himself as a king. He wears a crown on his head and regal rings on his fingers. His bed and his chairs all are regal in their adornments. His servants treat him like a king. People cannot approach him. He puts them down. In his mind what he is doing is right, for after all, what is a king! Some kings have been idiots!

Willie wanted to see peace between the USA and the USSR. He liked Jews. He would say that they are an amazing people. They are always busy, doing things, getting things done. He also liked the Russian people and especially their writers and poets, such as Dostoevsky, Chekov, Tolstoy, Pushkin.

Willie never forgot that he was Armenian. He was proud of that despite the fact that Armenians had given him nothing, nor helped in any way. It was Jews who had given him opportunities and helped him get ahead. He would say and write, "Some people like Armenians, and some don't. But I am one of those Armenians."

Willie's Last Words

I parked my pickup at the corner of Clinton and Fresno streets, in front of the Veterans Hospital. Willie had gone many places with me in that pickup. Getting out of my truck I walked slowly to the hospital entrance, and took the elevator to the fourth floor.

I was walking along the corridor toward the room where Willie lay. I heard a nurse calling out, "You can't go there. No permission!" But I ignored her and continued to room 404. Just at that moment Mihran's son Reuben was coming out of Willie's room. He said, "Not now, Varaz. The doctor is with him." I said that it made no difference who was with him. We were talking a little loudly, and Willie recognized my voice. It seemed he got new strength and with his still booming voice he called out loudly, "Let him in. Let Varaz in."

I entered quickly. Willie was lying in bed. Three thin plastic tubes were connected to his body. He was getting his nourishment intravenously. Standing there was Dr. Artin Jibilian. Willie introduced me to him. I greeted him but we had known each other for years. I asked Willie how he was feeling. He said, "Varaz, I'm dying. I'm dying." I said, "Willie, my dear friend. You are not dying. You're not going to die. I'll give my blood so they can operate on you." He said, "No, Varaz, I don't want to live. I don't want to live."

I said, "You will live. You will live forever. You have given us such writings that you will live eternally." He said, "That was thirty-five years ago. Varaz, I wish you good health."

He turned his head away, and in a moment turned back and said, "Varaz, again I wish you good health, health and a long life of creativeness." Again he turned his head to the other side.

Those were his last words.

Those were the last words he spoke with a mortal tongue. After those words no audible sounds came from his lips.

The next morning, at 6:45, May 18, 1981, at the age of seventy-two, he died. He was my best friend, Willie, whom I still mourn.

That morning I was standing there, all alone, for an hour, along-

60

side his body. There was no one else there, not even those who would be interested in his will. Yet, such people even bothered him during his dying moments, especially his son. He bothered Willie about trivial things. Willie had had some of his books brought to the hospital so that he might give them away to the nurses. But Aram had taken them, and would not permit them to be given away. Willie had been very much annoyed at that and had sent Aram away.

I was watching that lonely, melancholy giant of an artist. He had said, "I know that every man must die, but I shall not die." And yet, this talented man, this genius, my friend, had also died. But in the end he did want to die, and depart from this vain world.

He had wasted away physically. He was a skeleton, the size of a child. His left eye was partially open, as I stood there looking at him. It seemed perhaps he wasn't dead after all, but poised midway between life and death.

Willie had died physically, but his works keep him alive. As in ancient Egyptian philosophy, when man lives and breathes, he exists, but as long as his created works exist, he lives.

I left him. I phoned Osheen Keshishian in Los Angeles immediately so that he would telephone Armenia and inform the people there of the sad news.

The news of his death spread across America. It flashed on television screens. CBS newscaster Dan Rather announced it this way: "William Saroyan has died. He was a man who said that all men must die, except for himself. And today he too died, at seventy-two years, in Fresno."

SAROYAN

1908 - 1981

The following words were printed in Varaz Samuelian's "1979's Sketch Pad (Watercolors, Pen and Ink Sketches), translated by Bob Der Mugrdechian.

I am publishing this book in memory of my most beloved friend William Saroyan (Willie).

With these few words I don't wish to praise his being a great, creative writer because his writings are plain to behold. For the past fifty years he and his works have been praised by readers, highly regarded writers and critics alike. He will be praised for centuries to come.

I want to say that at 6:45 in the morning of May 18, 1981, at the age of 72, the people of Fresno and the United States and the entire Armenian nation and the whole world lost one of the 20th century's great persons and writers. And I, in addition, lost my inseparable friend of 25 years.

Cruel death separated us from one another but death is only a barrier.

"Go, Willie, let your ashes rest lightly and be scattered over America, Armenia and all the corners of the world." Goodbye and perhaps we will be exceptions and maybe meet in the next world.

Other Books by Varaz Samuelian

History of Armenia and My Life (1978)
Neutron Bomb (1978)
Poems and Stories (1978) in Armenian
1950s Sketch Pad (1980)
Circus (1980)
Contemporary Art and Short Stories (1980) in Armenian
The Art of Healthy Living and the World of Tomorrow (1980)
    in Armenian
Disaster—The War (1981)
Money (1982) in Armenian
Memories of Trip and Poems (1984) in Armenian

greetings from
Fresno, Armenia;
Erwan, California —
friend gourken Mahari;
great mardyros Serian
family; and to all of
friend
willia
Saro

For Varaz Samuelian
of the Sassoune
favit of the Art World
& San Benito Avenue
Fresno
with great admiration
& wishes for more &
more new works (never
mind the slow & lazy
response of the people)
from
Bill Saroyan
Fresno November 4 1964

For my f
from Arme
Varaz Sa
great artist
much m
continued go
sincerely
william